STELLA G.

DANCES

Original Pieces for Piano
Book 4, Rev. 2

To my family, friends,
and all who love music.

Acknowledgments

I am grateful to my family and friends for encouraging me to create this book.
Special thanks to Fredrick Allen Williams.

Music Engraving by
George K. Mohammed

Music is the soul of the Universe

It comes to us first as a lullaby and

Stays with us until our last journey

Music is a devoted friend with whom

We can share a palette of different emotions

From lonliness to ecstasy

Music escorts us from the haunting Past

Through the realized Presence

To the mysterious Future

1. Christmas Medley

arranged by Stella Gaukhshteyn

Rock Beat Boogie

Andantino

2. Sailors' Song and Dance

Stella Gaukhshteyn

Dance

Moderato

3. Spooky Bumble Bee

Stella Gaukhshteyn

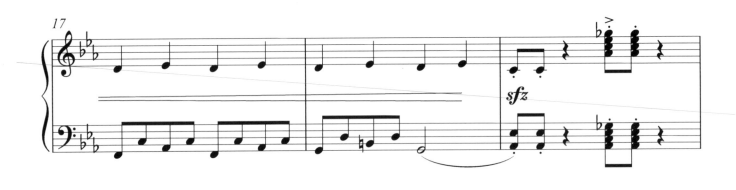

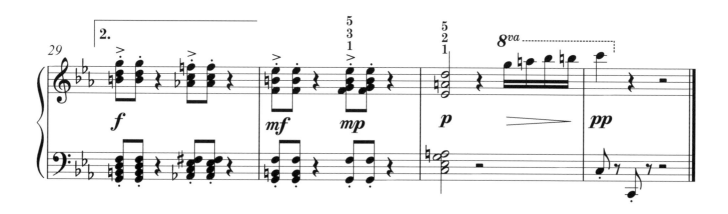

In memory of Zina Gershberg

4. Tango Reminiscence

Stella Gaukhshteyn

5. Waltz Dreaming of You

Stella Gaukhshteyn

Dedicated to N. Stefanova

6. Tango Revelation

Stella Gaukhshteyn

Energetic steady beat.

con anima

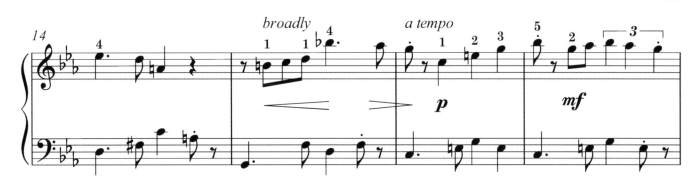

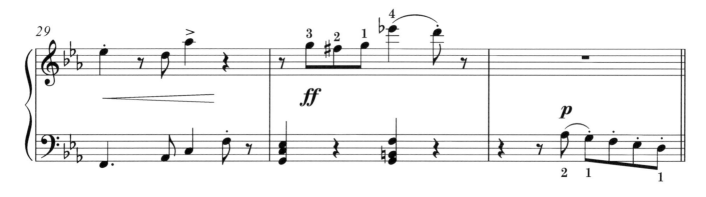

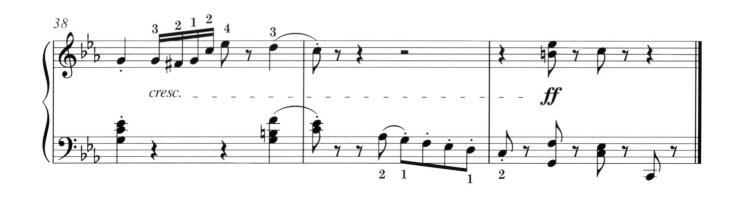

7. Spring Waltz

Stella Gaukhshteyn

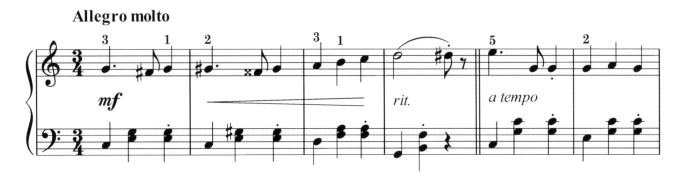

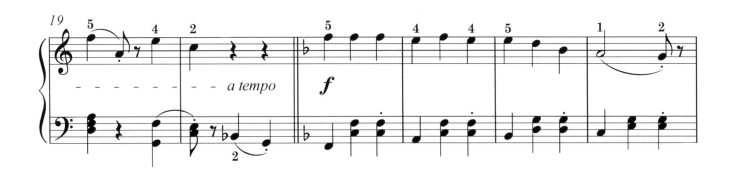

8. Hanukkah Medley

arranged by Stella Gaukhshteyn

Allegretto scherzando

Allegro moderato

Slower

Maestoso

9. Funny March

Stella Gaukhshteyn

34

SGD409/R2-34

10. Awakening of the Forest Fairies

Stella Gaukhshteyn

Made in United States
Orlando, FL
23 August 2022

21403676R00022